Unearthed, Tracy Ryan's seventh full-length collection, shows the poet at her mature and forensic best. Dominated by an elegiac sequence of poems for her Swiss-German first husband (from whom she was divorced and who has since died), *Unearthed* unsparingly analyses Ryan's unresolved grief — and the ambivalent feelings that remain from the severing of any intense relationship. 'Now you are dead perhaps we can really talk,' she proposes in 'The Sleeper'. The final thirty pages of *Unearthed* offer a series of elegies for dead friends, some poems about her present family's joyous, if somewhat embattled, life on a 'Vegan Block' in rural Western Australia — and a couple of extended elegies, impressively translated from Lamartine and Rilke.

Ryan's attention to craft is seen not only with her finely tuned sonnets and a villanelle but also through her increasingly characteristic couplets and quatrains, reinforced by cleverly irregular rhymes. Once again, Ryan reveals herself as poet with both a clear sense of tradition — and a contemporary understanding of Ezra Pound's old injunction to 'Make it new!'

— *Geoff Page*

Tracy Ryan was born in Western Australia but has also lived in England and the United States. She has worked in libraries, bookselling, editing, and community journalism, and has taught at various universities. She is especially interested in foreign languages and translation.

Previous poetry titles with Fremantle Press include *The Argument, Fremantle Poets 1: New Poets* (editor), *Scar Revision, Hothouse, The Willing Eye, Bluebeard in Drag* and *Killing Delilah*. Tracy Ryan is also the author of three novels: *Sweet, Jazz Tango* and *Vamp*. Her work has been commended in the National Book Council Banjo Award (1997), shortlisted in the Western Australian Premier's Book Awards (1994 and 1998), in *The Age* Book of the Year Award (2008) and the Adelaide Festival Awards for Literature (2012). She has won the *Australian Book Review* Poetry Prize (2009) and the Western Australian Premier's Book Awards (2000 and 2012).

Visit Tracy Ryan at poetsvegananarchistpacifist.blogspot.com

UNEARTHED

TRACY RYAN

FREMANTLE
fine independent publishing PRESS

CONTENTS

CONTENTS

UNEARTHED

TRACY RYAN

FREMANTLE
fine independent publishing PRESS

OTHER ELEGY

THE THOUSAND GOODBYES

for John

Love, if I presume on
your sad patience
caught in these threnodies
for past relations

Think of Dad who'd always
sit in the car and wait
after we'd been visiting
already out late

Running the engine
and tapping the wheel
as Mum from the window
continued her spiel

Sighing, indulgent
though rolling his eyes
Women! — I call it
the thousand goodbyes.

KARLSRUHE

KARLSRUHE

KARLSRUHE

Do you remember Karlsruhe?
We pitched one night there
Heedless, on our way elsewhere
Though I couldn't describe or

Find it again now. Chosen
For name alone, like sticking
Pin in map, or scrying:
'Your rest' a good omen

Because journeys must be broken
Though they seem seamless.
That any point's potential is
The end, we didn't know then.

Now if I could wake you up
From this last rest, this incubus:
Turn, *schau*, there's the corner pub
That, random, admitted us

Nameless as love. Was the room warm?
Your hands were, and your cheer
We ate potatoes, drank beer
Went upstairs to the dim

Deep privacy of what's forgotten
Our space, our time, relished and wasted
Till with morning, well-rested
Without let or hindrance, we moved on

As if there were always more
Where that came from,
And not this blank to answer for
This calling home.

THE SLEEPER

Und dann kamest Du.

Hattest wie Dornröschen schlafend gelegen ...

— KM

1 Liebestod

Wraith-man, Toggeli, coming to wake me from life
into dream, dragging, soothing, *You are my wife*
and so I was, but the dreamt-you has forgotten
the twenty years that followed: decrees nisi and absolute,
remarriage and two children. Mephistophelean,
you come to make your claim, and come again
and each time, for the dream's duration, Sandman,
I accept the bargain, *This is where you belong*, am lulled,
see them receding, my little family, love you only, how could I not
remember, of course, walking death-wish, O much-older but
none-the-wiser, first stakeholder, first foot in the door before
the wicked fairy's prick came into the picture,
and we know where it went from there.
Dawn and I'm bolt upright, reach to touch the real, the solid
second husband, fifteen years now – doesn't that
dispel you? – see his chest rising and falling, my head
above water, but when I sink once more, you lure me
back to our house that floats, continent
adrift, intent on merging with ancient landmass:
what do you want? Life's blood on a plate? Acknowledgement?
My guilt. This limp sack of guilt I become, I bed down on,
night after night, my curse, to recall each detail
of our days, our downfall. I could sleep for a century

and never have done with this spectral reconstruction:
not gorse and thorns but native restitution. Inside
the hedges, that house lies as it was, the same size
though the green your hands planted has grown,
grown up as I did not then, frozen, Dornröschen, Helen,
or Gretchen. So grown that no one can see in.
Now you are dead perhaps we can really talk.

2 Proof

Two years I fought those dreams and then I looked
          you up and you were dead. Two years too late.
You came like news on ships in former times
          or like the stars' far light, already out.
I dig and sift for what might be lodged here,
          weighing you down, as if we were pure
archaeology, and bringing to light
          were some sort of answer, a talking cure.
Here is a photograph you took of me
          nowhere exactly, somewhere in between,
en route to Paris in a spartan car:
          the Orient-Express. Where had we been?
Myself asleep, a classical riddle:
          The one perspective I can never have.
Asleep fully dressed, because you kept watch
          so I could let go, with no inkling of
your need to pin the moment, or the cause:
          affectionate impulse, or need for proof
of ultimate surrender? – what I was
          when all sham fell away, myself, *your wife*.

3 Spätlese

Ever the sweet tooth
you lived on fruit
I drew you with
bonne-bouche I couldn't

help, comfits and treats
easy as breathing
you took my baits
– it had been so long

so late this letting
out, intoxication
(and I knew nothing)
an initiation

tasted *a liquor*
never brewed, swallowed
there on the soft sand
came back for more

sly grog, you said, or
they'd take it from us –
nothing outrages
like May-December

let's keep it low-key
free as the daisy
Brassens was adamant
mustn't be put

in the marital stewpot
but I was insistent
we tied the knot
the petals were spent

he loves me
she loves me not
now public property
for every pot shot

you had one foot in the
grave, they'd snigger
sugar daddy
father figure

side by side we slept on
odd couple in cuckoo clock
safe in our winding down
nothing could wake.

4 *varium et mutabile semper/femina*

(Virgil, *Aeneid* 4: 569–70)

The world will always welcome lovers – but
not if they're old or ugly, same in sex
or differing in skin-colour or age.
True, lovers always think some evil hex
or imprecation meant for them alone
hangs high above them, singling them out.
You feared attack, yet that came from within.
Who is so safe as we? says Donne, without

belabouring the point's flipside: that *we*
who idolise may also desecrate.
I watched you lie like Dido on the pyre
I stopped my ears and left you to your fate.

5 Spell

You lay sidelong, silent behind me, on those white sands, first sands,
moulded to my young body as if you could encase me, your hands
the hands of a cellist, maybe (legs around me), trying a new instrument
but silent, so silent. I did what you said, went where you went, learnt
the little death, the huge release, both of us homeless and making a bed
in each other's hollows – you were grass, the whispering grey of your hair
and your skin smelt uniquely of eucalyptus, I would know its faint note anywhere
and I did in the dark when at last we had our own house, that cabin of sweet red
cedar that likewise disclosed its scent when sun beat on timber by day
and by night we were ravelled and tangled in such deep slumber, we lay
till with morning the parrots had stripped choice hips from the roses,
under our doors the small frogs hopped and scorpions reared powerless
because nothing could rattle this aestivation, hibernation, sweet soporific stasis,
lotus-eating we gloated, luxuriated as if fuel were endless, as if I could always
find my way back to the bed in the dark by your voice's sonar, as if you would
always be there to chafe my poor feet back to life in your broad
sure hands.

      Now you lie nowhere exactly: ASHES REMOVED BY REQUEST OF FAMILY
– I am no longer family – and so with ineluctable vagrancy you choose to visit me,
nightly, dropping in, overriding all that has come since and between, and though
this poem may seek to break the spell, I wake and murmur: *do not go.*

OFFERTORY

Even this house, years later,
has hotspots, risky pockets

I alone can locate,
no trouble to anyone else;

vestigial organs never thought of
till inflamed, and whose complaint

I must now swallow,
another man's wife;

tomb objects I alone
interpret, because it's me they follow

to this floating afterlife
insistent in their domestic

materiality, small
unexploded ordnance like

the lethal war-leavings
you warned me of

near the wild beach where
we once swam naked

and which is now
built over — *development!*

How you hated that word
that meant its opposite.

You wouldn't know
my world now

but these things have
survived you, these only,

indifferent and ordinary:
that hole-punch, a blue stapler,

two of the gilt-edged dinner plates
we got – always skint –

with coupons, one chipped
and one intact,

tiny Zürich spoon which I regret
has lost its mate,

flyleaf note in the complete
correspondence of Dylan Thomas,

wallet-sized studio-shot from your youth
the back of which grants *Rapperswil*

but nothing clearer,
a few short video moments

of our last day together
at someone else's wedding –

is it enough, is it proof?
If you insist like this

I don't know where
you can settle, scattered

like shrapnel which was always
your favoured name

for small change, and if
it's words you're after:

a line – just one – from a poem
you wrote when we first met,

which if nothing else
I ought to have kept

but still, the line has caught,
a private reference

I can't translate.

FOOD ODE

Love's way is through the stomach. — German proverb
The way to a man's heart is through his stomach. — English proverb

When we first met I would bake up
your own oatmeal cookies, the coarsest
grain, intent on bringing you back again
each afternoon, a talisman.

When you moved in, it was apple cake
as requested, first day after work,
strewn with thick chunks, green skins
left on; you couldn't stop,

gobbled the lot, your thin frame
bulked out at waist like the snake
digesting, mystery picture
that opens *The Little Prince,*

till you groaned, *I am paying*
for the sin of gluttony,
but smiling and unrepentant,
tearing your pleasures

with rough strife
as Marvell suggested.
And so it went on: cool velvet of ripe
avocado you topped with vinaigrette,

spoonfed till I was speechless,
complicit. I'd never tasted it.
Dark Sumerian bread that showed
aged and crusty outside

but sticky and lush within,
blackberries spreading a trail
of eager fingerprints on skin,
hot home-made onion tart that lifted

the roof from impatient mouths,
even those Moreton Bay figs
I swore were not edible (wrong)
and the mountain

of mangoes you strove through
like a responsibility
to bliss, when we found them
in Brisbane, too cheap to resist.

Somebody had to do it ...
On and on like this,
the fresher, the rougher, the better
till I knew why in her letter

my once-sad friend Isabelle said
Since we married we've both put on
a little weight, and didn't care one bit.
Die Liebe geht durch den Magen.

ARTICHOKE

So many folds, a luscious mystery
peeled off in layers, deepening
as you reach the centre – bland, one-
coloured, on the outside, but the trick
is in the subtlety, the barely-there,
flower of communion, teaching how,
hot, stripped and dipped till we have
the core, the choke, the heart of the whole
hungry matter, somehow
never sated, the eating more about method,
more in what we seek than what
we find, and so we start another
and another, the same act over and over.

KARTOFFELPUFFER

Each morning from pan to plate
the way you taught me

though they don't know that,
this man, this boy

a different story
a different language

theirs is the eating
not the history

not the particulars
of how we got there

by trial and error
to match your mother's

because food's always better
the way it was

seasoned only
with deep investment

and how we arrived
at the simplest:

I must resist the wish
to adulterate, nothing but

grated potato and
hottest oil possible

mastering fear and
impatience at once

withholding my touch
till the fringes crimp just short

of burn, like a leaf
on the turn, then over.

That love is pure heat
and confidence

I can never master
but must keep tending

little cakes like augury:
if they stick, they predict

how the day will go;
but no, they slip neat

as anything meant
to continue, lifting

the best from the past and
offering, making it new.

UNEARTHED [1988]

1. Poem for Karl

How like the rain
seeming indifferent to season
reason need wish want demand
you come along
timely or not, matter-of-fact, showering
life, death, as circumstances suggest.
You accept what you find on arrival
proceed by your own logic
clean as gravity, water-clear.
I could not win you by dance
or by incantation
but still you came.
You find love as easy as falling.

2. Fragment and reconstruction

They say that years later, after losing a limb,
old sensations haunt the wounded man.
He feels an ache in the arm that is long-gone;
it seems still a part of him.

When I am torn away from you ...

That's what I wrote in nineteen eighty-eight;
the rest is forgotten, but it followed suit.

These are the old sensations: here, and here,
left where you chafed and petted at my hair

and chest until at last you fell asleep,
brush of your stippled beard against my nape

soft as a broom that wears the shape of all
it's swept, your warm expansive mouth, the feel

of one gold tooth, the tongue, the tang of breath,
coffee and cheese and bread, your throaty laugh,

the rare surprise of a rich baritone
on those few times you sang, your mute tension

holding off pleasure, eucalyptus-scent
of armpit and neck, the wild dry fringe that dipped

over the mole on your brow; the furrows there
I'd yet to understand. The lines end where

the poem is torn away from memory,
blazon of air, itself a phantom body.

TRANSHUMANCE

You came down from an alp out of *Heidi*
in my head, your head still in the clouds.
Yours was another era altogether:
self-sufficient, Swiss provision
against disaster, a well-stocked cellar.
Here in a dry world you pulled
up greens from the roadside
the way Spyri's young Peter ate sorrel
or drank milk fresh from the goat, like
birthright. People said *eccentric*
because you took what you found
where you found it.
Ripped up armfuls of fennel, dill,
mint, blackberry that still grew wild
though heavily sprayed – when I tried
to say *You can't eat that*, you declared
them the same you knew as a child:
everything there for the taking, nature
to you could never be tainted. In you
persisted something unassimilated,
something neither *never no way* New
Australian nor *Eidgenosse* but dispersed
between points of the journey, eternal
return, defiantly migrant despite official
certificate, someone for whom home
could only be earth-simple, Alm-Uncle,
at odds with both God and man yet quite
certain of meadow, of mountain.

THE HOMECOMING

That month apart, bleak Advent, northern hemisphere winter
but for me a month of drought, I spent touring the phone boxes
of Europe, pouring my remnant cash into cards that
were never long enough, homing from Lourdes or Siena, faithless
pilgrim, filling in time till your own leave kicked in –

what a mistake, thinking to make the most of my longer
holidays, carting the dull ache of your absence everywhere I
went – every foreign word took on your accent – and the nights
peeled off like ballast till you could take that plane so we were just
twenty-four hours more out of range, Christmas Day the only date

you could get because we booked late, plane empty so staff plied
you with drink, carols & treats, clocking a fellow lost soul, not knowing
your ship had docked at Fremantle on Christmas Day just like this
a quarter-century before, you meaning to turn your back on the old world
for good, exactness uncanny as omen, any more than you could

have known you'd ever look at Zürich again, luggage lost
via Amsterdam so that you showed barehanded, old man like the new
migrant you'd once been, *naked I came from my mother's womb
and naked I shall return.* When I took the train to meet you
at Zürich airport we fell together like anxious hands and swore

never to do it again, it was wanton, insane, to waste, to take for granted
one moment, not worth one glimpse of Romanesque, of Gothic, the world
had nothing to offer we didn't already possess, our blissful hubris, like
taunting God to do his worst, we would not even go out to eat that night –
better the four walls of the Family Room they'd earmarked me at the hostel

'for when your husband arrives', quitting the shared girls' dorm,
but when we turned the key the beds were still only single, and bunk-form,
and there was no question but to fold ourselves into one, to lay us down,
unmoving, like the parts of an instrument packed in a snug velvet case,
coffin-dark, each in its place at peace and meaningless in isolation.

FREIENBACH

Nothing is as it was.
I must take your word for it –
your earlier village
lost like a dream image.

Peaked roof above churchyard
where your parents are buried,
you swear was once an onion-dome.
Each chiselled name was face and form

to someone. I am following on
as you take this path
through moss and marble
like so many stepping stones

crossing a stream, free to roam,
free as Freienbach, here
where you were born.
You insist, It was bigger then!

in memory's disproportion.
The forest is lopped by half,
makes way for an autobahn.
Fir-deep, the small hovel

that housed a man and wife
with elephantiasis
you, six perhaps, would spy on
hidden from everyone

coveting their self-
sufficient isolation –
is gone. Why should the earth
stay put if we abandon?

Now only you can trace
the truth of these features
like an old woman
mourning her unlined face.

It is others who age.
Others who die. We know this,
the headstones' exegesis.
Nothing to do with us.

Eros out for a walk
with Thanatos, *Liebes*,
the word cast off
flimsy as skin cell, helpless

as illness, beginning
the day we draw breath.
Only the change is sure:
there is no cure,

·

Gottfried, Elisabeth, each parent
mere cipher to me on the document
that stamped us married
here real, laid side by side.

I have seen their pictures:
sober, devout, historic;
anyone slightly wild, let alone
their own child, could not

but disappoint.
You loved them both.
You looked like neither
father nor mother.

He was a teacher, she
a Hausfrau
who burned her family papers
for fear of Hitler

crossing the border. You never
knew more, nor asked her,
strict Catholic whose maiden
name was Jewish.

When the call came,
you did not mention it;
for days you were oddly quiet
then at a public dinner, burst out:

I cannot *feast* when my mother is dying!

Despite your outcast status
she left you, *defrocked priest!*
unbeliever! your own fair share
which bought the ticket back,

back, to Freienbach, far too late.
It's always too late.
She was laid in the shadow
of an onion-dome no longer there

and you stood, a grown son,
to pay what respects you could
thirty years estranged, set root
on the other side of the world.

You told me she always said:
In life we may only move forward.
And now you too are dead.
And nowhere visited

but in my dazed head:
I do not know where
they have put him.
Nothing is sacred.

Why am I still sad
these years later, when all
of your tales are told, what more
can you leave me, teach me?

No more of that cyclist so gross
his wife must make easement
in the seat of his pants, a wedge
of fabric that never matched,

to help his belly out.
He was the village rich man
but still she had to patch.
Never mind Lazarus.

No more of that priest who so loathed
the parish votive lamp he enlisted
you, small boy, to help dump,
midnight, in the lake, so he could vamp

his chapel up, mad modernist
rid at last of the tasteless lump
till the villagers, out boating, spotted
its glint in the murky deep

A miracle, *Gott sei Dank!*
and dragged the old lamp back.
No more of the sandy banks
that rimmed the lake.

The lake is still, the boat
has long since sunk
along with the pebbles you'd skip.
When my time too is out,

who will dredge these stories up?

GÖSCHENEN

I remember no town, only mountain
no sky, only summit

as if at the outset defining
a limit, a crushing sublimity, the moment

we stepped from the train
so steep and immediate it pressed

the breath from us, sucked up all colour
sheer vertical, black and white only

rock and snow and no room for
negotiation, presaging a fall

as I stared once when small at the school
flagpole till the world seemed to waver

poor stand-in for peak or spire
and in class to make a point you'd sketched

a village just like this, generic,
mud map I picked up and pocketed

after the rest had gone home, kept
as a patch of your dreamscape and nightly

reanimated, set stories there till the inside
of my own head took on those contours, I crossed

the slopes, heart's cradle, like the alpine
garden the grandmother pictures

that isn't literal, that means heaven
but that Heidi keeps looking for

in this world. It was New Year's
Eve and we had the hostel, Alm-Uncle,

all to ourselves, but for the old couple
who managed it, who let us in and let

us be, unjudgemental, impassive as
that colossus that overshadowed us

yet at midnight they knocked and wanted
to raise a toast: *Your health, your health,*

that is the most important thing! said
nodding at you so knowingly but it meant

nothing to me then, too young, I smiled –
das ist das Wichtigste – and drank it in.

DUAL CITIZEN

1 Pass

Jus sanguinis, law of blood,
         as if by transfusion
you lived on, involuntary vampire,
               I carry
by former marriage a mantle
you never wanted –
         Swiss Australian –
wherever you lived,
         you did not belong,
             were the black sheep,
             scapegoat.
Is this what you
             impart, what I
       inherit?

2 Assisted Passage

Lobbed across continents
with a sweetheart on the SS *Sydney*

COME TO SUNNY AUSTRALIA!

             no word of English but
this is the house that Jack built

lodged in a Nissen hut,

                           set to cut

lengths of metal

            for a suitcase company

in a country that didn't rate

immigrant degrees,

               making a new start.

3 Homeless

Later, when all fell apart:

                        off out of the

Marital Home and all alone,

                  cramming

into your Charger,

      lairy car she called the *death trap*, dossing

on back seat, teacher now – my teacher

                          for a while there

though I didn't know where

            you were living

         planning your classes and marking

on front seat,

         washing in beachside blocks, moving on,

till when we met again

         in my twenties

                you'd holed up

in a caravan with just room enough to stretch out –

           how could I not let you in?

4 Expired

Red compacts, marked
with a little white cross,
   discarded,
      old entities
in the bedside drawer:
      am I still the bearer?
I own each particular.
Each unused LEAVE TO ENTER.

Acknowledge derivative status,
canton
   where I was never born
      and had never been,
cold northern town
of your first known ancestor
        mine
by assertion –
   a woman takes her husband's
Place of Origin, in the Swiss system –

handed on, in this wise
to my children's children,
   with no Swiss 'in' them,
IDs accreting,
   cancelled and slashed,
buried now among piles
      of underwear,

sketches for a portrait, Wildean,
that cannot flatter;
   the stages of breakdown.

How lightly I thought to cast it all off!
There's this whole other apparatus
       that wants to track me,
my *representation*,
that notes all my sins in the context
   of civil status
      and translates them.

5 Origins

Bülach, Bürgerort, is up near the border
almost off the map.
I've no real business here, revisiting,
kicking down streets I barely remember
   and that never knew me.

You hadn't been there either,
just learnt by rote the family lore:
Place of Origin means
   if we are ever destitute, we claim
   this right: they have to take us in.

You were always losing your foothold,
the very roof over your head,
      your good
schoolmaster-father,
   Swiss-village pillar

somehow ruined,
                         so that when we toured
so many years later, you showed me
two childhood homes: Before and After.

Then on to the school for boys
who 'sensed a vocation', under the chill
watch of that Black Madonna,
                         her foot
kissed so often it had worn down
like a patient child,
                         bearing Einsiedeln,
place of the hermit,
                         alone in a crowd.

6 Absolved

You were vowed to the Lord
                         and enrolled
to spread his Word:
                         Missionshaus,
Maria-Enzersdorf, in Vienna.

Always Maria,
substitute mother.

                         When they expelled you
after many years
                         (you who'd been telling
townsfolk *Priests can't really forgive your sins*)

you went back to find your cell stripped
and reassigned.

For months you slept
in an attic, fed by a soft-hearted nun
who brought secret plates from the kitchen
that was trying to starve you out.

Did you think of Bülach then,
with nowhere to turn,
knowing that shame meant your parents' door
was closed forever?

7 Outsider

The real Bülach is starkly quiet as
I scout around it,
looking for
nothing. I head across town
and a young man,
thinking me English, warns,
'But Fraülein,
that is the *Catholic* church!'

MOTHER TONGUES

Most of the time we lived in mine
or appeared to

you had been here as long as I had,
arrived in my birth-year,

but had to wear it in
second skin

(your sixth, if we count
unspoken Classics)

though there was always
a tacit understanding

we could call on yours
and it erupted, comic hernia

in the shared gut of our daily
dealings, at times of great

frustration, bemusement or when
words failed you.

At uni the man who ran
the language lab said, facetious,

that's how they catch spies
get them to count or say

times tables, you can always
trip up a mother tongue

coax it, shy animal, or
smoke it out, too brutal.

I pull on the tip and up
comes a whole scarf, colourful,

knotted to others and
not about to stop, a magical

evisceration but I want
all of you, things you have

names for that aren't
seen here: *Zwiebelturm,*

Trachten, Bergbahn –
or fragments, foods from

childhood, still stuck to their
labels and longed for

though irretrievable:
Hagebuttenmarmelade,

so that we cook up together
a *Wähe*, a *Brei*

because *die Liebe geht durch*
den Magen – goes through the stomach

like language, and last but not least
the cloud of names

buzzing about my head, like Pigpen's
dust but unseen by others,

unmerited, since I could not live up to them
and they sound now, so many

years later, nearly obscene
with lost intimacy:

Süsses, Schönes, Gutes,
Schatzi, Putzi, Liebes.

THE DRIVER

You said: *One person cannot own another.*
You drove me there and waited in the car.
You knew it didn't matter what he wanted.
You guessed he wouldn't pay the taxi fare.

You served him dinner and you heard his stories.
You knew he wouldn't stay and couldn't last.
You read him as a temporary measure.
A necessary evil and soon past.

You thought you had to leave the front door open.
You saw he wasn't worth your least bootlace.
And when the moment came and I was done with
You calmly cleaned the vomit from my face.

COURT

Crowded, as if it were a public meeting
or some austere worship session
of the Protestant sort, no ornament.
If anything, tedious.
Just slightly embarrassing, being
stuck en masse with others like us
who've met the one-year-separation
minimum, and want to move on, no fuss.

No stepping forward, lines to learn,
vows to explain away, a day
wasted on plastic seats, averting eyes
till names are called, names dissevered
or resolved, precipitate from murk.
Everyone tried to make it work.
Now it's our turn, a quick one
there being no child of this union.

No *issue.* Now we can go, unjudged
and undone, no fault, no hurt except
that it's so short compared to how we got
into it, and the fee six times as much.

THE PAWNED WEDDING RING

Like the promise it signalled: not kept.
Out there like space junk, no way to track
its course or luck, or how many more
fingers it might have graced (*O for the touch*)

no hallmark to speak of, featureless
standard issue of suburban jeweller,
cheapest in shop, & in return
for the ninety you'd winced over

I got merely thirty, like pieces of silver
but it was gold, however minimal,
however hard-won, was genuine,
and how it haunts me now

– was it all worth so little?
Less to me then, as I burned my already
shaky bridges, than clinker, than tap washer,
lightly on and lightly off

reduced to function, to calculation,
to liquidation, laid like a trap
for the next indigent
ready to take her chance, slip on

and does she ever wonder
who cashed it up with such
insouciance, imagine perhaps
the death or widowhood

we never made it to, at least not
together, not bound, handfasted
relieved of this little item
I can never redeem

because it has long since moved on,
innocent of regret, cold metal that yet
burns in the second skin where it is
welded, unshiftable as Cain's mark

or witch's, clamping the *vena amoris*.

DURAL WAY

Stalking my own past
on Google Street View:
the lawn is in patches now
grevilleas bare
all those weekends
you raked and watered
made no difference
to the big picture
twenty years later
but I temporise –
we'll to the woods no more

In silence, in distance
I pursue this,
nervous of tampering, as if
Sehnsucht left fingerprints, as if
staring could conjure us, you,
back into existence,
and this mess were only
so many stitches
to gather, to knit up,
so many parts of a tangram
I could force patterns from
but who could read them?

I turned to share the transport
– Oh! with whom ...?
Home has become abstraction –
what was unique, generic
into the garden once hidden
any browser may look
but hindsight is mine
alone.

TRANSLATION LOSS

Like someone hit
by a truck
or a stroke

it seems I can
no longer speak
German, that part

closed over
when we ceased
to talk

a permanent
glottal stop
that hurts like

knives in
the throat
I met a friend

who shares
all your languages
which became mine

in turn
or so I thought
but when I sought

words for him
they choked up
stilted, like sobs

WATER-GETTING BY MOONLIGHT

... daß wir nicht sehr verläßlich zu Haus sind
in der gedeuteten Welt ...
– Rilke

I've left it too late, this chore
so normal I'd not think twice –

tapping the source that shores
up our attempt at house,

small supply we set
such store by, not yet

plumbed in, so I take this route
a dozen times daily, noting

volume and purpose, use
or waste the way others

might watch expense.
So easy to sink

as if it weren't finite.
I mete it out, to make it last

as John gets wood in winter;
Tim calls me Water Woman.

It's part of my whole routine.
But never by night, meaning

to keep mosquitoes out
for the sake of Tim sleeping,

so that this one occasion seems
wild and untested.

Commonsense insists
it's the same set of actions,

that I've just become staid
or timid, ensconced in the lit,

the domestic, afraid.
There is the moon you taught me

to read, that cursive A to Z
that in your own tongue indicated

waxing or waning, *abnehmend,*
zunehmend, but inverted

here in the new world,
underworld. I'm walking the dark side:

your same old orb near-full,
mood-pull and cycle in its thrall,

casts a pall over the still
house so the slab-path,

tombstone-flat, is split
into halves like phases.

Halves of a life that meet
and fade as we round corners.

You wanted a home
just like this, little Walden.

But this is our idyll, not yours, better
late than never. This is the water,

the fall we drink from, new enough
to be trusted, innocent of silt,

making a fresh start.
The old tank has sat and sat

unclean, fit to burst,
forgotten past, a cyst.

We wash from it because skin
is forgiving, but can't drink

it in. Both tanks by moonlight
made over, a muted silver, not

plated, dead, or ossified but
transfigured, understood

in another idiom. To work by
this light, I must accept or

tolerate a loss of star-field,
different bearings, diminished

yield, the constellations
not as I knew them. But what

a moon you bequeath me, ribbing
the corrugations till they gleam

and ring as I knock softly
half-full, half-empty.

NEXT

Who will I be when I no longer feel this?
I've had too many griefs not to know
the way they go, the way they settle down
as the earth settles on an old and unmarked grave,
only there if you know what to look for,
barely a dent in the world's thick skin. Yes,
even this, though once we were *next of kin*.
How will you sit then, mere name
no longer on lips, nor even written – return,
then, will you, as last gasp, my deathbed confession?
Unknown to my children, who must assume
I utter nonsense, or am wandering. Less
than a whisper, all our time's truth, my youth,
my first, my former, what did it mean, *till death*?

LAST WORDS

The last time you came
in a dream
          you sat beside me
on the brick ledge
          of a flowerbed
in an unknown town

You said
At last you will hold my hand
          in public!

Taken aback, I said
I was never ashamed
          but don't you understand
          you're dead?

Your face was shocked, you unhooked
our fingers – said, embarrassed,
          I had no idea.

RECOVERY ROOM

No more dream visitations:

            you've *moved on*,

as they say,

        little by little knitted in

like tissue,

       like dissolving stitches;

                not needed,

the terror of memory

          thrust on like

an oxygen mask

     I don't want,

         some floating hand

insists before I

      come to.

      I push it away.

REHABILITATION

I have enrolled
to pick up *that language*

again. I sit in the group
and watch

each rounded noun pop out
from other mouths than mine,

not jagged, not brute
but light on the lip,

retrieved from the merely
private, and find

I can take them in
and give them back again

like my son
starting to cough up what

small water he might swallow
learning to swim,

and breathe again, fluently,
coming to no harm.

Not to be struck from
your idiom, flinching and dumb.

Nobody cares if I make a mistake.
The thing is to speak.

THE DISENFRANCHISED GRIEVERS

Everywhere, secretly, they speak another tongue,
these ones who must dissemble and keep up

because they cannot cut the truth to suit
or act Lot's wife made good, assimilate

among the citizens of our sweet state.
They do not even talk between themselves

about the unnamed baby lost or taken,
about the funeral they were not at,

remaining family who count them out,
embarrassed and impatient to rewrite

the life-that-was. Gay lover, other woman,
first wife or husband, facts we can't digest.

They should not feel like that, they have no right.
They should be over it by now. The mere

existence of their plaint is out of joint.
They made their bed and won't lie still in it.

Each word we force-feed rings only echoes
beyond our hearing; the contract says

they must spare us affront, and so they do,
but it's a part they play. At heart they're split

between two time zones, with their own watch set
upon another hour they must translate

to keep abreast. And we can't even tell
by looking, theirs is just the face we wore

a moment when we bore some uncouth news
we somehow tidied up because we could.

Yet they insist, their whispers growing loud.

BRAG BOOK: SEVENTEEN YEARS

One more time I must cause you pain
and then you can rest – bear with me if I boast
of what's worth having – see these images,
this house so like the one you yearned to build
this wild, thick bush, this hill, this man, this child.
Often across the years I thought: he'd love
to see this; if he did, he'd understand.
Once more insensitive, I plead my case,
not that it justifies mistakes we made, I'm not
that cruel, no *felix culpa*, but at least
I haven't flagged, I've kept the faith, I've found
love of the sort you taught me and still further,
the largesse of life that can give twice over.

OTHER ELEGY

Alphonse de Lamartine

THE LAKE

And so, forever driven toward new shores,
Borne off in endless night never to return,
May we not for a single day cast anchors
     In time's great ocean?

O lake! the year has barely turned around,
And near the treasured waves she should be seeing
Again, I come alone to sit on ground
     Where she was sitting!

You roared like this beneath the deep-set rocks;
Like this you smashed against their ravaged side:
Like this, the wind tossed your waves' foam across
     The feet I adored.

One evening – do you recall? – we sailed
In silence, hearing nothing between waves
And heaven but far rowers' rhythmic sound
     Striking the waters.

Suddenly accents unknown to the earth
Of this enchanted shore struck up echoes;
The waters paid heed as these words came forth
     In her cherished voice:

'O time, call off your flight! O kindly hours,
            Abandon the chase!
Allow us to savour the brief pleasures
            Of our finest days.

Plenty of wretched here ply you with prayers:
            Roll, for them – roll on;
Take, along with their days, their gnawing cares;
            Leave lovers alone.

A few more moments – but I ask in vain,
            Time escapes in flight.
I say to the night, "Go slowly", but dawn
            Will dispel the night.

Let's love, then, let's love – in the fleeting hour
            Quick to take our bliss.
Time has no far shore, and man no harbour;
            It flows, and we pass!'

Jealous time, can these rapturous moments,
When love pours us long floods of ecstasy,
Be blown away from us just as fast as
            Days of misery?

What – can't we at least fix the trace of them?
What – gone forever? What – entirely blank?
This time which gave them and erases them
            Will not hand them back?

Eternity, oblivion, past time –
Dark gulfs, what do you do with swallowed days?
Speak: will you return to us the sublime
         Bliss you robbed from us?

O lake! mute boulders, caves and dark forest,
You whom time spares or can make young again,
Keep, lovely nature, of this night, at least
         A recollection!

Keep it in your repose and in your storms,
Noble lake; in your hillsides' glad features,
And in these dark firs and wild rocky forms
         Hung above waters!

Keep it in the breeze that trembles, passes,
The sound of your banks that your banks repeat,
The silver-browed orb that pales your surface
         With its mellow light!

Let the moaning wind, the sighing reed,
Let the soft scents in which your air is clothed,
Embalmed, let all that's heard or seen or breathed,
         Let all say, 'They loved.'

ALYSOUN

Ich am in hire baundoun.
— 14th C. poem

Mother fierce as beast   large with love
Though a stinging tongue on you   equally sharp in hate
When called for   or when you wanted to
You should have been named Capability West
Made over every landscape
Nothing you couldn't get
The best of   and always on top of it
Whether at work redrawing the map
Of a whole community to make it tick
Writing a politician's speech
Or off on picnic with nanny and our two girls in tow
Feeding mine forbidden sugar till she vomited
Pink flood of candy floss
Knitting a jersey for yours to dress   as Dennis the Menace
And always acutely listening
Dogged, an ear cocked
For anything you could take care of
Dragging your tardis-handbag that brought forth
Apple or aspirin   sweetie or safety pin
Plaster or phone number   poem or bus fare
Before it was even asked for
Your catch-cry *Organised*
Coiffed with black spikes you passed on to your daughter
Calmly sluiced off the pot of yoghurt
She tossed in your face at dinner   petulant
Young lady   you'll only do that once

You'd trained her *Always fight back*
And you meant it   but not like that
You fought in the darkest corner
Your chuckle a spark that could break into laughter
Both loved and dreaded   never quite sure
Where it would land   *I hate nature*
You'd beam in the woods on a ramble
Hard Glasgow lass   appropriately scornful
Of Sassenach petty-glamour   the chocolate-box cuteness
You chose to live in   and would do the rounds of
Look for the nearest tea-rooms   order
Whatever we wanted   and you'd get it
Slinging your feet up on the next chair   and declare
This is the life

PICTURES, AS PROMISED

To David Musselwhite, Essex University literary critic and friend,
who kept asking for photos of our new place in wheatbelt Western
Australia but died suddenly, before they could be taken.

1

These are the lilies flushed with shocking pink
people call Easter lilies here, the way
names grow from usage, cling to what we say
they are, however tenuous the link

to language elsewhere. Sprung up in the chink
between the septic tanks, resistant clay,
marking a distance and a funeral day,
so far and so final. We always think

there'll be one more occasion, one last word
to fix the thing, to capture what was meant
clearing the air – not that we'll be cut short.

Rest of my life, the news you never heard,
and now, the images I never sent:
fading as light, the best of them uncaught.

2

This little room like a monastic cell
but for the cluttered paperwork and books
building around me till the whole thing looks
a living, breathing backlog. You can tell

the past in its accretions, this my shell
morphing to fit me, as a mollusc hooks
and holds – laid nacreous within the nooks
and crevices, your last few lines I well

recall: *I have spent too much time alone
and reading.* See: beside me on the shelf
your published works now all that I can find

of you, whose creations outlive your own
existence as a shell outlasts the self
soft-bodied – as ideas survive the mind.

3

Now for the 'guest room': note the concrete floor
where carpet has been stripped and not replaced.
Room of potential, doorway Janus-faced,
caught between what might be and nevermore.

Read it as empty nest – a daughter sure
of life elsewhere more suited to her taste
or a blank slate, a vacancy embraced,
room for imagining some new decor

we'll never settle on, a different air.
One wall a mirror, one wall looking out,
room to lie fallow, room where nothing grows.

Grey inner sanctum, Ely-niches bare
of all pretension, monument to doubt
and moving forward, picture of repose.

4
Three kangaroos. Quick – on the upper block
just by the driveway, feeding after dawn –
largely nocturnal, but they're sometimes drawn
to stay out grazing like a daytime flock

if they feel safe enough. For once the shock
is all on our side, stunned to stillness, torn
between desire to watch and urge to warn
them off – most locals here would mock

at finer feelings, shooting them for meat
or skins, or just for kicks. Yes, I feel shame
telling you that, but that's the world we know.

No time for photos now, as they retreat
soundless and blending in, the way they came,
too late, too fleeting, images let go.

5

Smoke haze above the Toodyay hills that just
a month or two ago would have meant fear
(seasonal, burning off the paddocks here)
colours are dull now, gold has turned to rust –

sights I would send you, ashes, dust to dust,
eternal return of the declining year,
this other world, your missing hemisphere.
Wherever you are now, you surely must

receive an intimation, as in dreams:
trees brown as northern autumns but they're dead
from lack of water, not deciduous,

roof of old farmhouse held fast not by beams
but bales of hay inside, a makeshift shed
proof of persistence: metamorphosis.

KELP

You could say he was Angus guitarless
because of the riffs hidden in him, rough and raw
tripping the inner ear, ready to roll somewhere but
unheard – rarely spoke unless to crack a joke
or an anecdote, curt and pointed at the absurd, he thought us
garrulous and spoiled, though he liked us. And because he was just that size,
that thin, with milky skin in his black tee-shirt somehow shrunken,
DBs in winter but bare callused feet in the heat, a crown
of brown curls that the Deputy itched to cut, till the tag took hold:
Would Kelp please come to the headmaster's office, Kelp
to the office please and the whole school knew
he was in for it, though innocent, because he always was –
ever the mate or brother-of, sidekick or henchman but nothing
aggressive in him, eyes blue as the chalk he used on his pool-cue
and that accurate, that mute. Eyes his one beauty, true to the mild
skies of his mother's Ireland, not like the stark Perth light,
not like the bright enamel of Yves Saint Laurent's *Rive Gauche*
he gave me, inexplicably, when I'd finally saved up enough
to book my flight to France, so that the mystery of that silent gift
went all over Eurail with me. Never had money except
if he won at The Dogs, but never nicked stuff either. Eyes that others
disparaged
with names he turned to humour, to his advantage, Froggy and Bullfrog
for the one lazy lid we'd never noticed, because as Sean said,
When you know someone well you don't really see them.
He was one of five like a shelf of canisters in descending size, people said
peas in a pod, wayward siblings, having to prove himself distinct

every time cops stopped to question him, keeping his nose clean,
couldn't help the resemblance, but to us he was unique, unmistakable,
only one who took the train to school because he lived so far,
one who dragged us, fanatic, to see *Kiss Live*, the night before
final exams so our heads were ringing, probable origin
of my now middle-aged part-deafness ... Who wandered off
in the darkness at Quarry Park while my brother got it on
with the girlfriend they hadn't let come between them, till Sean
was terrified he'd fallen down a hole or cliff, and had the cops out
searching at one a.m., till when day dawned we found him
asleep on the back seat of Sean's Torana, having hoofed it
maybe eight ks and finding the car unlocked, not wanting to knock
and 'wake us' in the house,
                         crashed out, clueless at all the fuss.

He never mentioned
Sean's death to me, not once, though he was there in the water,
and his own brother drowned a year later, it was not in his nature –
blows were just what you took, and you took them
and you took them, and then you took Ryan's sister
and girlfriend down to the fairground
on the Peninsula at Mandurah,
round and round on the Octopus till we were dazed with sickness
and you laughed and insisted on more,
came every Sunday dinner for over a year to take the place
of lost brother and son, always marvelling at how much we ate
because food for you was no consolation, just something
to get down when hunger pestered:
hot chips or sausage, corn jack, potato scallop,
pastie or Chiko roll, purely functional, like Cinzano Bianco
and Stone's Green Ginger Wine, no pretension,

just purpose, and even when off your face
you could pick the bullshit, could tell a deadbeat
from a dickhead but kept your own counsel over it
and if anything earned your approval it was merely *all right*

which is how I hope you would take this eulogy eighteen years
too late, if you could hear me, as you lie in Fremantle only a few feet distant
from Bon Scott, mascot of every Kemmy Rock, himself as wry and laconic
as your personal soundtrack, the hard kind of poetry you could hack.

REFLECTION

Fox flat in the right lane, neat as a cat
stretched for maximum heat
by a home-fire's grate – but cold
and growing colder, those moments before
rigor mortis, before metamorphosis
into effigy, into this travesty
of yourself

such plush and colour, such fire
gone out now but blazed on the retina
like eyeshine
as if you were still there.
I'd swear any minute you could rise
and dash to roadside, vanish back
into bush, my wishful thinking.

Yet as I return
an hour later, here you are
on my side now, become something
I have to remember, make room for.

FOX ABSENCE

Openings in the slope
rounded and dark as eyes
put out, no use musing
whether eviction or cunning

abandonment – peer as I might
I can't fathom the layout
of this den, *exits and entrances*, yet
I saw him once, dashing up

perhaps from my own sensed presence
fellow misfit, blurred, a thick
brushstroke I almost mistook
for a visitor, doglike,

catlike, but utterly non-domestic,
stealthily ranging the one block
there's neither bait nor gun on.
Now he is gone, gone

and there's only this covert den
to prove any such tenancy,
gaps to disrupt the steep incline,
image in memory.

BEE TREE ON VEGAN BLOCK

Not aromatic now,
wrong time of year
but the bees cloud and spout,
break away
like a solar flare, hotspot
the rest of the block seems to orbit
as if it were an image
we could appropriate, given
we let them go about
their business unhindered;
their sweetness will sit
untasted except by those
for whom it's meant

and yet in season the scent
inflames memory, imprint
of all childhood's honey
before the cruelty it came by
was understood, what we thought
there for us, like a found poem
milling with promise.

Natural yet out of place –
it's an old colony
rugged, unsightly,
none of the pat neatness
of the bee-box, contrivance
of hive. Inside, a relentless mess

of purpose, of energies
no other may harness.
Whether there's queen or genius,
you'd never guess –
it looks like chaos to us
keeping a measured distance.

WILD OATS

No matter who sowed, utterly profligate
it's we who pay for them every year, never quite

meeting the set date – frivolous cloth rewoven faster
than we can ever unravel, so pale

they seem to give out light, or trap it, paper,
quill-thin, no substance but the idea

of tinder, wick or taper, invitation to disaster, fuel
load around house, less dangerous even if left to lie there

but upright they would undo us, biding their time, and despite
battle and vigilance, there's a tall fringe niggling

at my window, like the narrow patch you always miss
when you shave blind, residual, unkempt, indicative

of tricky bits, slopes or prominences not easy to master,
things we might rather ignore, picking out the irregular,

the persistence, the nagging nearly domestic now,
masking snakes, what's more, like that day I had to wade

through them, chest-high, to read the meter, as if
I could balance the books, keep on top or at least

keep up with this: they are what falls to rise again, the return
of an age-old urge repressed but determined to win.

FOR JOHN, IN SICKNESS AND IN HEALTH

While you are gone this side of the bed
weighs so heavy it could capsize
so I counter the waste space where
you would lie with the book you were
reading, page still marked
with dust flap, our shared story, ready
to be picked up where the day left off,
resumption of duty to life, routine, habitual
postures refuting the stiffness, the props
of hospital, this real, and your clothes
still redolent of body scent so
my senses are lulled, like a child
arranging the spread of soft transitional
objects somewhere between mute
and alive, *fort-da*, I place your shirt
beneath my cheek and dream you home.

WEEDING

I inherited this mess
somebody else's choice
the slipshod bank shoring up
a buckled verandah

that mad portulaca not content
to knuckle its hoard of rock
but swallowing steps till it's crept
up to the house's very lip

only held back by the choke
of wild oat, clover, flatweed
from which I'd work
to liberate it

as 'good', as fire-resistant
remnant of bed an earlier resident
left, half-hearted, abandoned.
I have never gardened

except in the convent
where there was a moral on it
Eden or *Candide*
yet here it's laid out

as brute, as bare necessity
reducing fuel load
the house is haloed
by bush, incendiary

so I must do my bit
clear a path for the succulent
the drought-tolerant
rip all this tinder out

by the root, each damp clump
unearthed shockingly pubic
the truth of growth – I fear
what might well lie beneath

all this friable wealth
my gloved fingers loosen
at the cold foundation
power of life and death.

DIALOGUE, WITH BIKE

The sense of cadence
depends on what follows:
how sound might rise

after dying off
the kind of silence
that feels like restful

friendship, where you say
just what you need to
and what's unspoken

creates a rhythm
as in a poem
keeping step

even on slopes
so steep you park
at the top

and descend on foot
happy to wipe
each boot

and make no fuss
knowing the waste that
might be laid

by any wrong tread.
Cadence an ending, from
cadere, to fall, I tell you

the same root as
cadaver, but it's also
circular, like the recurrence

of a turn no cyclo-
computer can really measure
unique to each

person, each voice,
each rising question,
falling response.

RAMBLE

NOW EVEN CLEARER
– sales pitch on the crazed
and peeling cover, *1999*,
the year before I left there, spine
cracked open at Cambridgeshire
as if it were an old favourite,
as if things were stuck there,
premillennial,
clearer with hindsight,
you might say, but for me it's fading.
What am I looking for?
– set of coordinates that no longer
applies, journeys you've
made & I wish
to retrace – *road atlas*
they made me repeat
in the bookstore
back when I worked there,
laughing at my 'directory' –
décalage in the same language –
but whatever you call it, it sold
by the hundreds, & then the customer
returns, disgruntled – *my village*
is missing! – small blank, erratum
only a local would notice,
good for a refund, though presumably
they knew where it *should* be ...
Unlike me, who never knew

my place, despite the discount on
Ordnance Survey Maps, where I learned
to interpret *footpath* as purely rural, interrupted
with stiles like so many valves in
a circulatory system, ha-ha and sheep grid,
hedge and drystone, understood at last
with British mud why said path must be strewn
with boot-studding stones. *Generations have trod,*
have trod, have trod ... met the casual nettle and
its trite counterpart, the dock
I could never quite identify, so kept well back
despite absorbing routes in walkers' guides
I could always locate and recommend
but was never going to take, a poetics of opposites:
LAND'S END TO JOHN O'GROATS,
ST BEES TO ROBIN HOOD'S BAY,
fourfold like motifs in old folk songs,
the limits spread out, mental map,
but the one I liked best, that I pored over,
gorgeously morbid: *THE LYKE WAKE WALK,*
the one on which we all, sooner or later, embark.

VERTIGO

But when I let go thy hand, I stagger on a precipice
— Hazlitt

The ground beneath our feet is never sure.
This path leads nowhere, like a famine road:
one simple movement and we are no more

possessed of ourselves than the crumbling shore,
edge of abyss we take for our abode.
The ground beneath our feet is never sure.

Skirting the fall, we think ourselves secure,
safe in the gaps our silences encode.
One simple movement and we are no more

than promise gone back on, plans made before
compass could waver, weather could erode;
the ground beneath our feet is never sure

when to expect us, what our words are for –
dust unto dust – it cannot bear the load.
One simple movement and we are no more

certain of self than limestone at the core
eaten to sand and destined to implode.
The ground beneath our feet is never sure:
one simple movement and we are no more.

DOUBLES

I cannot express it; but surely you and everybody have a notion
that there is or should be an existence of yours beyond you. What
were the use of my creation, if I were entirely contained here?
— Catherine Earnshaw in *Wuthering Heights*

1
My late good friend was a twinless twin.

Didn't know till the age of eleven, when
on a visit to distant acquaintances
they hadn't seen since he was born,
his mother was asked,

'Where's the other one?'

It was only then she turned to him:
'We never told you ...'

                    At sixty-one
he wrote to me, 'It shocks me still.
Perhaps he lived and I have died.
Maybe somewhere he writes the book
I talk about, is happily married,
a steadfast father.'

                    Stuck with the work
of moving house after years in place,

he added, with characteristic smirk,

'This rather Borges-like fantasy
is not unconsoling. The bugger can do

the packing for me.'

2
I read in the news of twins who died
aged 92, within mere hours

of each other and from the same cause;
decades of life spent side by side,

brothers in fact and then by choice:
Franciscan friars, rejected by

the military for their sight:
one's bad left eye, the other's right.

Their dad, a doctor, had prayed for a boy
but 'the Lord fooled him and sent two'.

One was a talker, the other quiet,
but neither would say who was born first,

their feat of sameness tended like
the monastic garden they laboured at,

the little things that made it count:
the Hours they must have known by rote,

the Rule to which they gave their will,
private in life, now singled out.

3
Also the ones whose names were mere
repeats of babies lost before,

(*replacement child* we call it now):
Vincent van Gogh reading the tomb

that bore his name and own birthdate
one year before; Stendhal, or Beyle,

of several hundred pseudonyms
as if to self-proliferate

could make a man original
could banish repetition,

arriving as they did upon
a stage already set for them

to improvise: *Thank God You're Here.*

4

Or those who entered on the heels

of a mother's death, whether at birth
or its aftermath, over whom
a father's loss and fancy loom
the 'second Mary': Mary Shelley

in St Pancras cemetery
spelling the words on her mother's tomb

while still a child, later the same place,
willow-shaded,
    she'd lie with Shelley

body-double, never fully descended
from the womb.

5

Where do we end   and where begin?

You talk of strangeness in our skin
the difference   and the interface

tenuous, but all there is
tangled past distinguishing:

'till death', we say, *Bist du bei mir*
the tenor sings
                (if you're with me ...)

you wrap me round to stem the shock
that sets my body shivering

my father in the hospital
unmoving now
   except for hands

lifted my wrist and said, 'A vein
the same as mine,'
    then let it drop.

Twice he mistook me for a nurse –
'You're so much like my daughter.'

His wife of more than twenty years
slept on a makeshift bed beside

him in the ward and had to call
every time he tugged the drips

and bags and oxygen away,
so many nigglers at his flesh.

She felt as if a phantom limb.
He could not tell the nurse his name.

Where do we end and where begin?

Rainer Maria Rilke

REQUIEM FOR A WOMAN FRIEND

I have my dead, and I let them go off
and was amazed to see them so at peace,
so soon at home in deadness, so well-placed,
so unlike all the rumours. Only you –
you turn around; you brush against me, prowl,
want to bump into something so it rings
with your sound, giving you away. Oh don't
take from me what I'm so slow to learn.
I'm right; you are mistaken if you feel
stirred to homesickness by the slightest thing.
We change all this around, it is not here;
we shine it forth, reflected in the world
out of our being, as soon as it's discerned.

     I thought you much further off. I'm bewildered
that *you*, who've changed more than any other
woman, should be the one to roam, to come.
That we were shocked because you died, no, that
your brutal death so darkly cut us off,
ripping apart the before-and-after:
that's our concern, and working through it will
become our task in everything we do.
But that you gave yourself a fright and still
now are afraid, where fright holds no more sway;
are losing a piece of your eternity
by coming back here, my friend, here where

nothing yet *is*; that you are not grasping
infinite natures' rising like the day –
absent-minded, your first time ever in
the Universe, absent and half-engaged –
as you used to grasp each thing in this place;
that from the cycle which has received you,
any disturbance's mute gravity
should drag you back down into numbered Time –:
often this wakes me at night: housebreaker, thief.
And if I might say that you merely deign,
come out of magnanimity and plenty,
because you are so sure, so self-contained,
that you go about like a child, not scared
of places where harm might be done to you –:
but no: you're pleading. This gets into my
very bones, cuts across me like a saw.
Any reproach you as a spectre brought,
brought against me, when I retire at night
into my lungs, into my inmost parts,
into my heart's last and poorest chamber, –
such a reproach could never be as cruel
as this pleading. What are you asking for?

    Tell me, should I travel – is there somewhere
some Thing left behind that struggles along
after you? Should I go to some land
you never saw, though it was kin to you,
was like your mind's forgotten other half?
            to travel on its rivers, want
                and ask about old customs,
                    women in their doorways
                        when they call their children in.

I want to note the way they cloak themselves
in the landscape out of doors at the old
work of fields and meadows; want to crave
that they should lead me in before their king,
and want to tempt the priests with bribery,
to set me before the greatest statue
and go away and shut the temple gates.
Then what I really want, knowledge-filled, is
simply to look at the animals, so
something of their turning passes over
into my limbs; want a brief existence
in their eyes which hold me and slowly let
me be, peaceful, without any judgement.
I want to get the gardeners to recite
me many flowers, so into the shards
of lovely proper names I might bring over
a remnant of the hundred fragrances.
And fruit I want to buy – yes, fruit in which
the land once more exists, up to the sky.

For ripe fruits, they were what you understood.
You used to set them out in bowls before you
and counter their gravity with colours.
And just as you saw fruit, you saw women
and so too saw children, forced or driven
from inside into the shapes of their being.
And in the end saw yourself as a fruit,
took yourself out of your clothing and dragged
yourself before the mirror, let yourself
in up to your gaze, which stayed hugely there
and did not say: I am that; no: this is.
Your gaze was so incurious at the end

and so without possessions, truly poor,
that it no longer coveted you: holy.

    Thus will I remember you, the way you
placed yourself in the mirror, deep within
and far from all. Why else do you come here?
What words are you taking back? What are you
getting me to believe, that in those beads
of amber at your neck there still sat something
heavy, of a heaviness there never
is in the next world's pacified images;
why show me in your stance a bad foreboding;
what does it mean to explain the contours
of your body like the lines on a hand,
so I can no longer see them but as fate?

    Come here, into the candlelight. I'm not
scared to look straight at the dead. If they come by,
they surely have as much right to stay on,
linger in our sight, as other things do.

    Come here, we need to be silent awhile.
Look at this rose upon my writing-desk;
is not the light as timid around it
as over you: it too should not be here.
Out in the garden, not mixed up with me,
it ought to have stayed or gone back there – now,
how it persists: what's my consciousness to it?

    Don't take fright if I now understand, oh,
it's rising in me, I can't do otherwise,
I'll understand, even if it kills me.
Understand that you're here. I understand.
Just as a blind man grasps a thing all round,
I feel your lot and have no name for it.

Let us lament together that someone
took you from your mirror. Can you still weep?
You can't. The strength and onrush of your tears
are what you gave in exchange for your ripe
gaze, and were about to transfer any sap
into yourself, into a great existence,
that rises and circles, balanced and blindly.
Then an accident snatched you, the last
to befall you, snatched you from your greatest
progress, back into a world where sap *insists*.
Snatched you not quite; snatched only a part at first,
but on that part from day to day the real
grew fat, and became heavy, so hard that
you needed your whole self, so off you went
and painstakingly broke yourself out in
pieces, out of the Law, since you needed
yourself. So you levelled yourself and dug
from your heart's nightwarm soil the still-green seeds
from which your death would germinate: your death,
your own individual death to match
your own life. And ate them, your death's seeds,
like any others – like all others – ate its seeds,
and in you was an aftertaste of sweetness
you did not intend; you had sweet lips,
you who were so sweet in your desires.

Oh, let's lament. Do you know how your blood
came back, hesitant, reluctant – you called
it back – from a circuit unparalleled
anywhere? How, bewildered, it once more
took up the body's small circulation;
how, full of mistrust and astonishment,

it joined the placenta and suddenly
from the long journey back again, was tired.
You drove it on, you pushed it to the fore,
you dragged it to the open hearth, the way
one drags a herd of animals to the altar,
and wanted it to be happy at this.
You forced it, finally: it *was* happy,
came running up and yielded. It appeared
to you, because you were used to other
dimensions, it would only be for a while.
But now you were in time, and time is long.
And time goes by, and time grows big, and time
is like a relapse into a long illness.

    How short your life was, if you compare it
with those hours where you sat and diverted
the many energies of your many futures
so silently into the new child-shoot,
which once again was fate. O painful work,
O work beyond all strength. You undertook
it day by day, you hauled yourself to it,
and drew the lovely weft out of the loom
and used all your threads with a difference.
And still had heart enough to celebrate.

    For since it was done, you wanted your reward,
like children, when they have drunk bittersweet
tea that is said to be good for their health.
Thus you rewarded yourself, for you were
far from all others, even now; no one
could have thought up a reward to suit you.
You knew it. You sat up in your childbed
and before you, a mirror gave you back

all things, utterly. Now all that was *You*,
and wholly *before you*, and in the glass
was only the illusion, the lovely
illusion of every woman gladly
putting on jewels and combing hair, transformed.

Thus you died, as women once used to die,
in the old-fashioned way, in the warm house,
you died the death of women in childbed
who want to close up and no longer can
because that darkness that they also bore
comes back again, pushing forward, and gets in.

Shouldn't we nonetheless have rounded up
some wailing women? Women who will weep
for money, and whom we can pay enough
that they howl through the night, when all is silent.
Give me some traditions, customs – we don't
have enough customs. Everything goes, talked-out.
So you're obliged to come, dead, and here with me
make up the lamentation. Hear me lament?
I'd like to throw my voice out like a cloth
over the shattered pieces of your death
and rip at my voice till it lies in tatters,
and every word I say must go out dressed
ragged in this voice and feel the cold;
if all I did was lament. But now, I accuse:
not the one who drew you back from yourself,
(can't pick him out; he looks like everyone)
yet in him I blame everyone: the Male.

If somewhere a former child-existence
rises from deep within me, yet-unknown,
perhaps the purest childlife of my childhood:

I don't want to know it. I want to fashion
an angel out of it without looking
and want to throw it into the first rank
of shrieking angels who must remind God.

For this suffering lasts really too long,
and no one can do it; too hard for us,
the chaotic suffering of false love,
that, building on limitation like habit,
calls itself 'right' and flourishes on wrong.
Where is the man who has the right to own?
Who can possess what cannot last or hold,
what merely from time to time collects itself,
blissfully gathers, and throws itself away
again, like a child playing with a ball.
No more than a captain upon his ship
can keep a hold of Nike on the prow
when the secret lightself of her Godhead
suddenly heaves her off into the great
ocean wind – no more can we call out
to the woman who no longer sees us,
heading off as if by a miracle
upon a thin strip of her existence,
without mishap – he who called out would show
desire and vocation to do wrong.

For *this* is wrong, if anything is wrong:
not to increase the freedom of a love
by all the freedom we can muster in
ourselves. We have, when we love, only this:
to let each other be. Holding on tight
comes easily, does not need to be learned.

Are you still there? Which corner are you in?

You always knew so much about these things
were always so capable, went along
open to everything, like a day breaking.
Women suffer: to love means being alone,
and artists intuit sometimes in their work
that they will have to transform where they love.
You made a start on both; both are in That
which now distorts the fame it takes from you.
Oh you were far from that fame. You were not
for looking at, had quietly taken in
your beauty as one might draw in a flag
on the grey morning of a working-day,
and wanted nothing but unbroken work –
which is not done. Nevertheless, not done.

  If you are still there – if in this dark,
there's still a place in which your spirit can
resonate, sensitive, on the shallow
soundwaves that a voice, alone at night,
disturbs in the current of a high room:
Then hear me: Help me. See how we're slipping,
not knowing when, back from our onward course
into something we don't intend – in it,
we get entangled as we do in dreams
and in it we die, without ever waking.
No one is further on. It can happen
to any whose blood is raised to a long-term work,
that he can't go on holding it that high,
and that it falls under its weight, worthless.
For somewhere there is an old enmity
between ordinary life and great work.
That I might recognise and say it: help me.

Do not come back. If you can stand it, stay
dead among the dead. The dead are busy.
Yet help me with this – may it not dispel you –
as the most distant sometimes helps: in me.

ACKNOWLEDGEMENTS

Some of these poems were previously published in *The Age, The Australian Literary Review, Island,* the Max Harris Poetry Award website, *Meanjin, Naked Eye, The Night Road: Newcastle Poetry Prize Anthology 2009, Poetry Review, Southerly*, and jacket2.org.

Parts of this work are indebted to Kenneth J. Doka, ed. *Disenfranchised Grief: Recognizing Hidden Sorrow* (Lexington, MA: Lexington Books, 1989) and to Pauline Boss, *Ambiguous Loss: Learning to Live with Unresolved Grief* (Cambridge, MA: Harvard University Press, 2000).

ALSO AVAILABLE FROM FREMANTLE PRESS

WINNER

the
a r g u m e n t
{p o e m s}

t r a c y   r y a n

an extraordinarily sophisticated,
thoughtful book. Her best collection yet.
Dennis Haskell

Shortlisted, Adelaide Festival Awards for Literature and NSW Premier's Literary
Awards. Winner of the Western Australian Premier's Book Awards.

'In the best traditions of lyric poetry, her poems are supple, tough and deeply
moving; they display little and reveal everything, her superb technique working
a deep, unobtrusive burnish from which flashes an authentic and disturbing
passion. — *Alison Croggon*

'Her "argument" is argument in the older sense of the word, a discussion of the
self with the larger whole of a post-God world in which a pattern of "giving and
receiving" – human, natural and impersonal – provides a richness to our lives if
we have the courage to accept it.' — *Dennis Haskell*

ALSO AVAILABLE FROM FREMANTLE PRESS

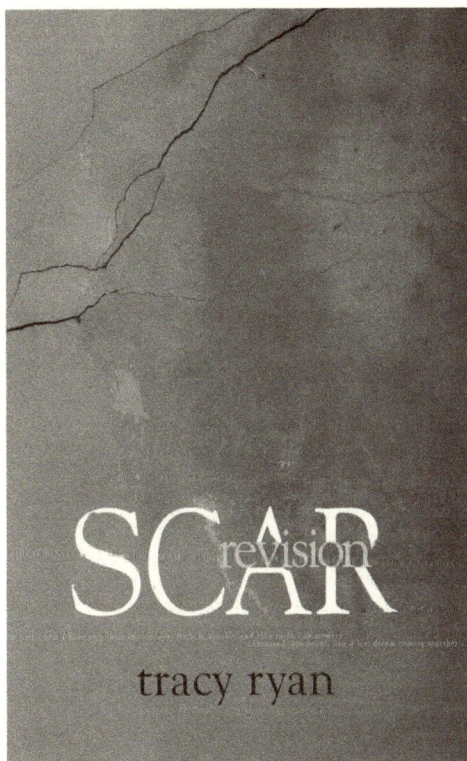

Shortlisted, *The Age* Book of the Year (Poetry) and Western Australian Premier's Book Awards.

'Scar revision' — surgically minimising the effects of scars — is the powerful central image of Tracy Ryan's highly accomplished collection. Both formally adventurous and movingly personal, these poems offer vivid accounts of how we survive and 'rewrite' literal and symbolic scars, and of regeneration through the risks of family.

'Tracy Ryan's poems are tightly packed vibrations of spiky conceits. They have a restless intelligence which seems to suspect everything they touch; the references are scholarly and the contention is feminist but the result is polychromatic.' — Tim Allen, *Terrible Work* (UK)

First published 2013 by
FREMANTLE PRESS
25 Quarry Street, Fremantle 6160
(PO Box 158, North Fremantle 6159)
Western Australia
www.fremantlepress.com.au

Consultant editor Georgia Richter
Cover design Ally Crimp
Cover photograph Claire Miller
Printed by Lightning Source, Perth, Australia

National Library of Australia
Cataloguing-in-Publication entry

Ryan, Tracy, 1964–
Unearthed / Tracy Ryan
1st ed.
ISBN 9781921888632 (pbk)

Australian poetry—21st century
A821.3

Government of **Western Australia**
Department of **Culture and the Arts**

lotterywest
supported

Australian Government

Australia Council

Publication of this title was assisted by the Commonwealth Government
through the Australia Council, its arts funding and advisory body.

www.ingramcontent.com/pod-product-compliance
Lightning Source LLC
Chambersburg PA
CBHW021149090426
42740CB00008B/1015